Tell ME What YOU Remember

PASTIMES AND TOYS

Northumberland Schools Library Service	
3 0132 02575097 2	
Askews & Holts	Oct-2019
S688 PURPLE	£7.99

Sarah Ridley

W
FRANKLIN WATTS
LONDON • SYDNEY

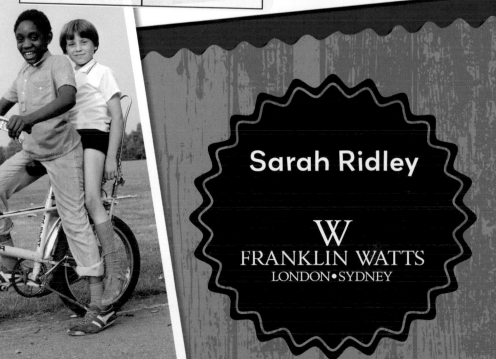

Franklin Watts
Published in paperback in Great Britain in
2019 by The Watts Publishing Group

Copyright © The Watts Publishing Group

All rights reserved.

Series editor: Sarah Peutrill
Series design: Basement68

The Author and Publisher would
like to thank everyone who has
kindly contributed their photos
and memories to this book.

ISBN: 978 1 4451 4364 4
Library Ebook ISBN: 978 1 4451 3979 1

Printed in China

Franklin Watts
An imprint of
Hachette Children's Group
Part of The Watts Publishing Group
Carmelite House
50 Victoria Embankment
London EC4Y 0DZ

An Hachette UK Company
www.hachette.co.uk

www.franklinwatts.co.uk

Picture credits: Peter Aves:
6, 20, 21b, 23t. Henry Grant/
Museum of London: 1, 17t. Hulton
Archive/Getty Images: 18b. Paul
Kaye Collection/MEPL: front
cover b, 12b. Kodak Collection/
Science & Society PL: 10b. Land
of Lost Content/Topfoto: 22t.
Picturepoint/Topham: 9t.
Topfoto: 4. UPP/Topfoto: 13tr.
Victoria & Albert Museum, London:
9b, 11c, 13tl, 15b. CC Wikimedia:
5b, 6t. WPL: 8b, 19t. All other
photographs are kindly given by
the people who contributed their
memories.

Every attempt has been made
to clear copyright. Should there
be any inadvertent omission
please apply to the publisher
for rectification.

Contents

Fun and Games

What toys do you play with at home? Do you make up games with your friends? Are you a collector or do you have any hobbies?

New toys and games are invented every year. The card game Happy Families was invented over 150 years ago and is still popular today. Other toys and games can only be found in museums or in people's memories.

Memories are what we remember about the past. Everyone has different memories about the toys, games and pastimes of their childhood. Talking to people about what they remember can help us to learn about the past.

Sue, born 1945, remembers...

I mostly played outdoors when I was growing up in the 1950s, but I did belong to Brownies. In this photo of my Brownie group we are trying to read the flag signals.

Mike, born 1967, remembers...

I loved my space hopper. It was a new craze in the 1970s and I spent hours bouncing about on it.

Teddy Bears

Do you have a favourite teddy bear or soft toy? Does it look like any of these bears? The first toy bears were made in 1902 in Germany. They had a hard body and soft fur made from goat hair.

Jessie, born 1940, remembers...

In 1944, I was given this teddy for my birthday. His arms and legs move on joints attached to his body. He has glass eyes. I made these clothes for him when I was 12.

Lucy, born 1970, remembers...

My mum read me bedtime stories about Paddington Bear. I also watched him in short films on TV. My own Paddington slept beside me in bed but I took his Wellington boots off first.

I loved the Care Bears. Bedtime Bear was my favourite. I spent my pocket money on Care Bear magazines and stickers and watched the cartoons on TV early in the morning.

Anna, born 1976, remembers...

FIND OUT MORE

Did your parents have a special bear or soft toy? Have they kept it? Ask your grandparents to tell you a story about their favourite teddy or cuddly toy.

Construction Toys

Babies and toddlers love to build towers using blocks or stacking toys. As children grow up, there are many different construction toys to choose from.

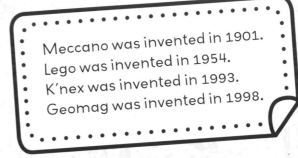

Meccano was invented in 1901.
Lego was invented in 1954.
K'nex was invented in 1993.
Geomag was invented in 1998.

Nick, born 1937, remembers...

MECCANO

YEARS OF FUN IN EVERY OUTFIT

TRADE MARK REGD.

I had a big set of Meccano, including a clockwork motor. At first I used the handbook to build models, but later I built cranes, bridges and other models without following instructions.

This photo was taken in 1964 when the Queen's mother was out on a royal visit. By the 1970s, many families had boxes of Lego bricks and children built what they liked with their Lego. Gradually more and more Lego was sold in sets with instructions to build a Star Wars spaceship or a castle, for instance.

Ben, born 1993, remembers...

My brother and I were always making things with Lego and K'nex. K'nex was quite a new toy in the shops. I liked K'nex because you could build vehicles powered by rubber bands.

325 pcs

K'nex

FIND OUT MORE

Compare modern Meccano and Lego with the sets that children played with 50 or 60 years ago. What is the same? What is different?

Transport Toys

During the Second World War (1939–1945), factories were busy making tanks, planes and other war equipment. With few toys in the shops, most children played with second-hand or homemade toys. New toys in the shops were often linked to war, such as a model plane.

Nick, born 1937, remembers...

After the war, my parents gave me a second-hand Hornby electric train set for Christmas. Like this boy, I spent hours making the engines move trucks and carriages around my rail network laid out on my bedroom floor.

David, born 1957, remembers...

My dad made sections of road for me to drive my model cars and trucks along. My favourites were Corgi cars because they were such good copies of real cars and had windows.

In 1969 the first men landed on the Moon. Toys inspired by space became very popular from then onwards. One of the most popular toys in the early 1990s was a Tracy Island model based on the TV programme Thunderbirds.

FIND OUT MORE

Did anyone in your family play with Scalextric or collect Hot Wheels cars? Does anyone in your family remember playing with train sets?

Hornby sold their first electric train set in 1925.
Matchbox cars were sold in small cardboard boxes from 1954.
Shops sold Corgi toy cars from 1956 onwards.
Scalextric began in the 1950s.
Hot Wheels cars were made from 1968.

Dolls

Children have played with dolls for thousands of years. They have been made from many different materials, including wood, wax, cloth, clay and china. After the 1950s, dolls were mostly made from plastic. From the 1960s girls could also play with fashion dolls, such as Barbie and Sindy.

Up until the 1960s, most dolls looked like babies or toddlers. These girls were photographed with their dolls in 1961.

In 1966 a new kind of toy arrived for boys called Action Man. This soldier doll came wearing his army kit. You could buy him a change of clothes, a tank, a jeep or a motorbike. From the 1990s, Action Man was more of a superhero than a soldier.

Lucy, born 1970, remembers...

One Christmas, I was given Tiny Tears. She cried tears if I fed her water. My granny knitted baby clothes for my doll.

Eliza, born 1999, remembers...

I had a few Barbies when I was little and a Barbie car. Later on, my friends and I preferred to play with Bratz dolls. Their clothes were more fashionable.

FIND OUT MORE

Ask your granny about the dolls she remembers. Why do you think toy makers started making dolls from plastic?

Imaginative Games

Children have always played games that they make up themselves. Some games need dressing-up clothes, a dolls' house or a wand. Other games just need a space to play in.

During the Second World War children often acted out war games on bomb sites or in their back gardens. Toy shops sold out of helmets and uniforms.

Here I am pretending to be a cowboy, like the actors in the films I watched with my parents on Sunday afternoons

David, born 1957, remembers...

Suzanne, born 1966, remembers...

I liked to dress up in my nurse's uniform. I cared for my little sister or my toys. My sister and I often made dens in the garden or behind the sofa and served pretend cups of tea to our cuddly animals.

Tom, born 1987, remembers...

My brother and I made up games with our action figures. We liked Power Rangers, Teenage Mutant Ninja Turtles and Transformers. They all appeared in cartoons on TV.

Transformers have been made since 1984.

Shops sold Power Rangers from 1994.

Teenage Mutant Ninja Turtles were very popular in the 1990s.

Teenage Mutant Ninja Turtles

Bikes and Trikes

During the Second World War, most bicycle factories were making weapons for the war and families could not afford bicycles anyway. During the 1950s, this gradually changed.

Jane, born 1963, remembers...

I rode a second-hand tricycle around the garden when I was young. Its three wheels stopped me from falling off.

In the 1970s, children longed to own a Chopper. Its new design made it a bestseller in the United Kingdom and in the United States of America.

James, born 1984, remembers...

My BMX-style bike was a birthday present. Older children could do all sorts of tricks on their BMX bikes.

FIND OUT MORE

About a hundred years ago, children started riding scooters. They were often made from pieces of wood and wheels taken from roller skates. What are scooters made from today?

Playing Outside, Clubs and Classes

When your grandparents were children, they spent most of their free time playing on the streets, in parks, in the countryside or at home.

Some children took music or dancing lessons. Others attended weekly clubs such as Brownies or Cubs, or went to the local swimming club.

Boys play football in the street in the 1950s. At this time, the football was made of leather. What do you notice about the street?

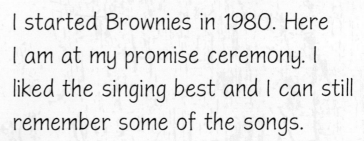

Sue, born 1945, remembers...

My sister and I took part in many village pantomimes in the 1950s. I am the smallest rabbit and my sister is the special fairy in this photo of our 'Sleeping Beauty' show in 1953.

Sarah, born 1973, remembers...

I started Brownies in 1980. Here I am at my promise ceremony. I liked the singing best and I can still remember some of the songs.

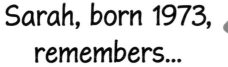

My mum went to a weekly club called the Girls' Life Brigade. Here she is in her uniform in 1948. Although it was linked to her church, the girls spent a lot of time keeping fit and entered skipping competitions.

Hobbies and Crafts

Growing up in the 1940s and 1950s, boys often collected things, such as stamps, coins or comics, while many girls enjoyed making scrapbooks and learnt to knit and sew.

Nick, born 1937, remembers...

Most of my childhood friends collected something. I collected stamps and coins. I also enjoyed making loud bangs and bad smells with my chemistry set!

Anita, born 1975, remembers...

I spent a lot of time drawing and painting at home. Mum often mixed up flour and water to make glue for me to do cutting and sticking. I also liked making pictures on my Etch-a-sketch.

A hundred years ago, many children collected cigarette cards as a hobby. Much more recently trading cards became very popular. In the late 1990s, children traded Pokemon cards in the playground and played Pokemon games on a Nintendo Game Boy.

FIND OUT MORE

Many children have always enjoyed reading as a hobby. Ask some adults which books they enjoyed reading when they were young. Have you read any of them?

Screen Toys

In the 1970s, some families bought their first home video consoles. Gradually, during the 1980s and 1990s, many more families owned video games or computer games, as well as the first hand-held games, such as the Nintendo Game Boy.

GAME & WATCH
Nintendo

OCTOPUS

AM 12:00

GAME A
ALARM
GAME B
ACL
TIME

◄LEFT

GAME A
GAME B

─WIDE SCREEN─

RIGHT ►

Tina, born 1974, remembers...

I had a Nintendo 'Game and Watch' electronic game in the 1980s. It only had one game, called 'Octopus'. Some of my friends had an Amstrad home computer. When we wanted to play a game it could take 10 minutes for the tape to load.

Timeline

Use this timeline to see at a glance some of the information in this book.

1901 First Meccano sets were sold.

1902 First teddy bears were sold.

1914 Brownies, originally called Rosebuds, were formed. Scouts began in 1907, Girl Guides in 1910 and Wolf Cubs in 1916.

1925 Hornby sold its first electric train sets.

1939–1945 Second World War.

1954 Lego and Matchbox cars were new toys.

1956 First Corgi models were sold.

1958 Paddington was published.

1960s/1970s Space toys became popular.

1960s Barbie, Sindy and Action Man became popular.

1966 Tiny Tears doll won UK Toy of the Year.

1968 Hot Wheels cars were new toys.

1970s Space hoppers and Chopper bikes became a craze. BMX racing was a new sport.

late 1970s/1980s Home computers and video games gradually became popular.

1980s Rubix's Cubes were a huge craze.

1984 Care Bears were first in the shops.

1990s Power Rangers, Thunderbirds and Teenage Mutant Ninja Turtles became popular.

1991 First Nintendo Game Boy went on sale.

1993 K'nex sets were a new toy.

2001 Bratz on sale for the first time.

2000s Scooters became very popular again.

2014 Loom bands became a huge craze.

FIND OUT MORE

Loom bands are a recent toy craze. In the 1980s, everyone wanted to have a go at solving the puzzle of the Rubik's Cube. Ask adults you know about the toys that became a craze when they were growing up.

Glossary

BMX Design of bike used for riding on rough ground or to do tricks.

Brownies Club for girls between the ages of 7 and 10 that is part of the Girl Guide Association.

Cigarette cards Printed cards inside cigarette packets.

Computer tape Computer games in the 1980s were recorded on magnetic tapes.

Craze When a toy or an activity becomes incredibly popular, often for a short period of time.

Girls' Life Brigade Church-based club for girls, set up in 1902 by the National Sunday School Union.

Handbook A book giving instructions or information about a particular subject.

Leather Material made from the skin of an animal.

Pantomime A Christmas show filled with songs, dances and jokes, usually based on a fairy story.

Rubik's Cube A maths puzzle toy, popular in the 1970s.

Scrapbook A book filled with photos, postcards, newspaper cuttings or drawings.

Second-hand Owned by someone else first.

Thunderbirds British TV series filmed in the 1960s using puppets and set in an imaginary space world.

Index